AMPLIFYING THE VOICES OF TEACHERS OF COLOR
THE NATIONAL BOARD CERTIFICATION JOURNEY

Dr. Rainya P. Miller, NBCT
&
Mrs. Simeona Stewart

© 2023 Consortium of Accomplished Educators, LLC. All Rights Reserved
This book may not be reproduced, in whole or in part, in any form without written permission from the publisher.

ISBN 979-8-218-29193-8(Paperback)

This is dedicated to my NBCT tribe, My family and the ones I love.

Table of Contents

FOREWORD

INTRODUCTION

CHAPTER I
The History of Teachers of Color in the American Educational System

- From Slavery to Reconstruction: Early Education for Black Teachers 7
- The Segregated Educational System and the Fight for Integration 9
- Contemporary Challenges and Opportunities for Teachers of Color in Education 11

CHAPTER II
Disparities Faced by Teachers of Color in the American Educational System

- Representation Disparities in Leadership and Pay 17
- Systemic Prejudice and Discrimination Faced by Educators of Color 18
- Addressing Disparities: Creating Inclusive Policies and Resources for Educators of Color 20

CHAPTER III
Achieving Equity in Education: How NBC Certified Teachers of Color Benefit Everyone

- Benefits to Educators: Advancing Professional Development and Leadership Opportunities 23
- Benefits to Students: Culturally Responsive Teaching and Increased Student Achievement 26
- Benefits to the Teaching Profession: Addressing the Teacher Diversity Gap and Promoting Equity in Education 28

CHAPTER IV

- The Journey of Accomplished Teachers of Color: Challenges and Triumphs 32

CHAPTER V
Enhancing Diversity in Education: Recruiting, Coaching, and Professional Development for Accomplished Teachers of Color

- Recruiting Accomplished Teachers of Color: Strategies for Equity and Inclusion 107
- Coaching Accomplished Teachers of Color: Cultivating Leadership and Growth 110
- TOC Professional Development Through Communities of Practice: Enhancing Teaching and Learning 112

CHAPTER VI
Concluding Thoughts

- Ensuring Success for All Teachers Through Targeted Support and Resources - Concluding Thoughts 121

ACKNOWLEDGEMENTS

APPRECIATION

CONTRIBUTORS

APPENDIX

FOREWORD

As educators, it is our duty to make sure that every kid receives an equitable education that will help them succeed in the real world. Regrettably, systemic challenges such as institutional racism and prejudice have contributed to the under-representation of teachers of color in leadership roles and among National Board Certified Teachers. This is a serious problem since teachers of color bring distinctive perspectives and experiences to the classroom that might be advantageous for all students. Amplifying the voices of Teachers of Color: National Board Certification Journey is a crucial step in addressing this issue. By elevating the experiences and perspectives of teachers of color who have successfully navigated the National Board Certification process, this book provides valuable insight into the strategies and triumphs that have led to success. This book also explores the history of teachers of color in the American educational system, offering a deep understanding of the systemic issues that have contributed to under-representation. I am honored to be a part of this book and to support the work of teachers of color in pursuit of National Board Certification. By amplifying these voices and offering strategies for success, we can improve the overall quality of education and work towards a more equitable future for all students.

INTRODUCTION

In a ground-breaking book titled "Amplifying the voices of Teachers of Color: National Board Certification Journey," teachers of color who have earned National Board Certification are given a platform to share their stories. In addition to interviews and a history of teachers of color in the American educational system, this book also offers advice on how to locate, recruit, mentor, and coach teachers of color during the NBC process.

In the continuing debate over educational equity, the perspectives of teachers of color are crucial. Despite the fact that teachers of color make up a sizable proportion of the teaching workforce, they are frequently under-represented in positions of leadership and among National Board Certified Teachers.

This book tries to solve this problem by emphasizing the experiences and viewpoints of teachers of color who have successfully completed the National Board Certification process.

Readers will obtain a deeper knowledge of the struggles, victories, and tactics that have contributed to success in the NBC process through interviews with NBCTs of color. This book also examines the history of teachers of color in the American educational system, providing insight into the structural problems that have led to the underrepresentation of teachers of color in leadership roles and among NBCTs. By amplifying the voices of teachers of color and offering strategies for success, this book aims to inspire and empower a new generation of NBCTs of color and improve the overall quality of education for all students.

This book takes readers on a journey through the stories of 16 National Board Certified teachers of color who have overcome adversity to become accomplished educators. These personal accounts shed light on the challenges and barriers faced by teachers of color in pursuing and achieving National Board Certification (NBC). Through their experiences, readers will gain insights into effective strategies for recruiting, coaching, and supporting teachers of color in their pursuit of NBC. Additionally, this book explores how the components of NBC can serve as a valuable tool for professional development among educators working with diverse student populations. Join us as we discover the triumphs and struggles of accomplished teachers of color and learn how to better support and empower them in the pursuit of their goals.

CHAPTER 1

The History of Teachers of Color in the American Educational System

FROM SLAVERY TO RECONSTRUCTION: EARLY EDUCATION FOR BLACK TEACHERS

The history of black teachers in the United States is complex and multifaceted, spanning several centuries. Teachers of color have faced a variety of challenges and obstacles, including discrimination, racism, and systemic inequality, since the early days of colonial America. Education was largely reserved for white, male students in the early years of the United States, with very few opportunities for people of color to become teachers.

One of the earliest examples of teachers of color in the United States can be found in the mid-18th century, when a group of free African-Americans in Philadelphia established a school. The African School was founded in 1787 by a group of African-American community leaders. It was one of the first schools in the United States to be founded by and for people of color, and it played an important role in the education of African-American children in Philadelphia in the late 18th and early 19th centuries.

The African School was established in response to the growing educational needs of African-American children in Philadelphia. People of color had few educational opportunities at the time, and many were barred from attending schools that were only open to whites. This lack of access to education was viewed as a major impediment to social and economic mobility for African-Americans, who were largely confined to low-wage, manual labor jobs. The African School was founded by a group of prominent African-American leaders, like: James Forten, Robert Purvis, and Absalom Jones. Robert Purvis was a prominent abolitionist and civil rights activist. Purvis was a key figure in the Underground Railroad and later founded the American Anti-Slavery Society. The principles of the American Revolution, which emphasized the importance of education as a means of promoting equality and democracy, inspired them.

The school was initially housed in a small building on Philadelphia's Sixth Street and was open to children of all ages and genders. Reading, writing, arithmetic, and other fundamental subjects, as well as religious instruction, were all part of the curriculum. Volunteer teachers, many of whom were members of the African-American Methodist Episcopal Church, staffed the school.

The African School quickly became a focal point of Philadelphia's African-American community, and its influence extended far beyond the classroom. The school provided a sense of community and belonging for African-American children and their families, as well as a sense of pride and self-worth in its students. In addition to providing education to African-American children, the African School played an important role in the fight against slavery and discrimination. Many of the school's founders and supporters were outspoken abolitionists, and the school itself became a symbol of African American resistance and resilience in the face of oppression.

The African School remained open throughout the early nineteenth century, even as the fight for civil rights and equality became more intense. As the abolitionist movement gained traction, many African-American leaders began to shift their focus from education to political activism, and the African School gradually faded from use.

The Segregated Educational System and the Fight for Integration

In the late nineteenth and early twentieth centuries, teachers of color faced significant barriers to entry and advancement in the field of education in the United States. These barriers were rooted in racism and discrimination and were reinforced by a variety of social, political, and economic factors.

One of the most significant challenges for teachers of color during this time was a lack of educational opportunities. Many African Americans, native Americans, and other people of color were barred from attending white-only schools and were frequently denied basic educational resources and support needed to become teachers.

Additionally, teachers of color were frequently subjected to workplace discrimination and harassment. They were paid less than white counterparts and were frequently denied professional development opportunities and other forms of assistance.

Despite these obstacles, many teachers of color persevered and contributed significantly to the field of education. Mary McLeod Bethune, who founded the National Council of Negro Women and advised President Franklin D. Roosevelt, was one of the most notable examples. Bethune was a tireless advocate for African-Americans' educational access and opportunity, and she helped to establish several schools and educational programs across the country. Booker T. Washington, who founded the Tuskegee Institute in Alabama and was instrumental in the development of vocational education programs for African Americans, was another influential figure in the history of teachers of color. Washington was a firm believer in the power of education to lift people out of poverty and oppression, and he worked tirelessly to increase access to educational opportunities for African Americans.

Other notable teachers of color during this time period included William Monroe Trotter, who founded the Boston Guardian newspaper and was a leading advocate for civil rights and racial equality, and Carlos Montezuma, a native American physician and educator who worked to improve health and educational outcomes for Native American communities.

Despite the numerous challenges they faced, teachers of color played an important role in the development of the American educational system during the nineteenth and early twentieth centuries. They left an enduring legacy through their advocacy, leadership, and commitment to excellence, paving the way for future generations of educators and students of color.

Contemporary Challenges and Opportunities for Teachers of Color in Education

The mid-twentieth century saw significant advancements for teachers of color in the United States. Following the landmark decision in Brown v. Board of Education by the United States Supreme Court in 1954. After the Supreme Court ruled that segregation in public schools was unconstitutional, opportunities for teachers of color began to grow in many parts of the country.

The National board of certification Journey

Despite this progress, teachers of color continued to face significant challenges and workplace discrimination. In practice, many schools and districts remained segregated, and teachers of color were frequently subjected to lower pay, limited professional development opportunities, and hiring and promotion discrimination.

Even with these challenges, many teachers of color made significant contributions to education during this time. Dr. Martin Luther King Jr., who was not only a civil rights leader but also a teacher and educator, was one of the most influential figures. King was a firm believer in the power of education to transform individuals and communities, and he worked tirelessly to increase access to education for African Americans and other marginalized groups. Gloria Ladson-Billings, an African-American educator and scholar who has made significant contributions to the fields of critical race theory and multicultural education, was another notable teacher of color during this time period. Ladson-Billings has been a leading advocate for educational equity and social justice, and she has contributed to a better understanding of how race and racism affect students of color's educational experiences.

Kenneth Clark, an African-American . psychologist, who played a key role in the Brown v. Board of Education decision, John Hope Franklin, an African-American historian who documented the history of segregation and discrimination in the United States, and Ruby Bridges, an African-American child, who famously integrated an all-white elementary school in New Orleans in 1960, were other influential teachers of color during the mid-twentieth century.

Although teachers of color faced numerous challenges and obstacles, they played an important role in the struggle for educational equity and social justice during the mid-twentieth century. They helped to expand access to educational opportunities for students of color and paved the way for future generations of teachers and scholars from diverse backgrounds through their advocacy, scholarship, and leadership. Their legacies continue to inspire and inform the work of educators and advocates who are dedicated to making the world a just and more equitable place.

The persistent achievement gap between students of color and their white peers is one of the most significant challenges that teachers of color face today. Despite efforts to close the achievement gap, students of color continue to lag in important areas such as graduation rates, standardized test scores, and college readiness. This can pose difficulties for teachers of color who work with these students because they may face higher expectations and greater pressure to produce positive results in the face of system barriers and inequalities.

The National Board of Certification Journey

Another issue that teachers of color face is a lack of diversity in many schools and district leadership positions. While there has been advancement in recent years in terms the representation of teachers of color in the workforce, this progress has not always been mirrored at the highest levels of educational leadership. This may make it more difficult for teachers of color to advance in their careers and have a say in decisions affecting their students and schools.

Today, teachers of color continue to make significant contributions to education. Many are actively involved in efforts to promote equity and social justice in schools and communities, as well as in developing innovative strategies and approaches to support students of color's academic and social-emotional needs.

Some teachers of color, for example, are employing culturally responsive teaching practices to better engage and support students from diverse backgrounds. Others are working to create curriculum and teaching materials that reflect the diversity of their students and communities, as well as to encourage critical thinking and analysis of race and social justice issues.

Furthermore, many teachers of color are working to establish relationships with families and communities, as well as to create inclusive and supportive school environments that foster student success and well-being. Teachers of color are helping to shape the future of education in the United States by providing all students with the educational opportunities and support they need to thrive through their leadership, advocacy, and commitment to excellence.

CHAPTER ii

Disparities Faced by Teachers of Color in the American Educational System

REPRESENTATION DISPARITIES IN LEADERSHIP AND PAY

There is a significant disparity in the number of black teachers in the United States and the demographics of the students they serve. In the 2017-2018 school year, 79% of public schools' teachers were White, while 7% were Black, 9% were Hispanic, and 2% were Asian, according to the National Center for Education Statistics. In contrast, the student body was 47% White, 15% Black, 27% Hispanic, and 6% Asian. Several negative outcomes for students of color have been linked to a lack of diversity in teaching.

There is also significant disparity in the representation of teachers of color in leadership positions. While 49% of students in public schools are people of color, only 20% of principals and 13% of superintendents are, according to the Education Trust. Because of this lack of representation, it can be difficult for teachers of color to advance in their careers and create a shortage of role models for students of color.

Finally, Black and White teachers are paid significantly differently. According to the National Education Association, the average salary for White teachers in the 2019-2020 school year was $59,800, while Black teachers earned $52,000, Hispanic teachers earned $48,800, and Asian teachers earned $54,400. Teachers of color may find it difficult to make ends meet as a result of this pay disparity, leading to higher rates of teacher turnover.

Systemic Prejudice and Discrimination Faced by Educators of Color

Racism and discrimination against people of color in the teaching profession have a long history in the United States educational system. Despite the progress that has been made, there are still many obstacles for people of color who want to pursue careers as educators. One of these issues is the "Black tax," which refers to the additional responsibilities and liabilities that teachers of color, particularly Black teachers, are expected to take on within the school system.

In addition to the "Black tax," educators of color face a variety of other forms of bigotry and discrimination in the classroom. Micro aggressions, such as the assumption that they are not as qualified or competent as their white colleagues, or that they are only hired to meet diversity quotas, may be directed at them. They may also have fewer opportunities to advance in their careers because they are frequently passed over for leadership positions in favor of white people. This could be another obstacle they face.

Besides that, children of color may have negative attitudes and biases toward their teachers of color, which can present additional challenges in the classroom for these educators. The lack of representation of teachers of color in the educational system can contribute to the perpetuation of these stereotypes, which can lead to the belief that teaching is not a viable career option for people of color.

Black educators frequently have to juggle the dual responsibilities of teaching and addressing racism and other forms of discrimination in the classroom. They may be asked to address concerns about racism and bias in the classroom, to serve as role models for Black children, to act as liaisons between Black families and the school. This additional strain can take a toll on their time, energy, and emotional well-being, threatening their ability to successfully teach and assist their students.

ADDRESSING DISPARITIES:
Creating Inclusive Policies and Resources for Educators of Color

In order to address the concerns raised, the educational system must acknowledge and address the systematic prejudice and bias that teachers of color face. To achieve this goal, it may be necessary to develop policies and initiatives in both the hiring process and the classroom that promote diversity, equity, and inclusion. It could also entail providing educators with training and resources to address racism and bias in the classroom.

Moreover, it is necessary to provide specialized support and resources, such as mentorship programs, professional development opportunities, and financial aid, to people of color who work in the teaching profession. This can help to alleviate the burden of the Black tax and provide teachers with the resources they need to teach and support their students as effectively as possible.

It is critical to provide a platform for educators of color to share their perspectives and testimonies within the educational system. To achieve this goal, opportunities for teachers of color to interact and network with other educators of color, as well as share their own narratives and experiences, should be provided. This can help to foster a sense of community and support among teachers of color, as well as inspire more inclusive and equitable policies and practices. Both of these outcomes may be advantageous.

To summarize, individuals of color who hold teaching positions continue to face barriers and discrimination in the American educational system. The Black tax, in particular, places an additional burden on Black educators, which may impair their ability to successfully teach and support their students. To address these issues, it is critical to recognize and address the systematic discrimination and bias that teachers of color face, as well as to provide targeted assistance and resources to help them succeed.

The teaching profession must become more inclusive and diverse. This can be achieved through targeted recruitment and retention efforts, such as financial incentives, leadership opportunities, and mentoring programs for teachers of color. It is also critical to provide opportunities for professional development for all teachers in order to foster cultural competency and a positive classroom environment. Finally, it is critical to address systemic biases within the education system and provide equal pay for all teachers, regardless of race or ethnicity. If we work together to create a more equitable education system, we can give all students a chance to succeed.

CHAPTER III

Achieving Equity in Education: How NBC Certified Teachers of Color Benefit Everyone

BENEFITS TO EDUCATORS:
Advancing Professional Development and Leadership Opportunities

The field of education is constantly evolving, and teachers are at the forefront of these changes. To ensure that students receive the best education possible, teachers must continuously improve their knowledge and skills. National Board Certification (NBC) is a rigorous certification process that recognizes accomplished teachers who meet high standards of performance. For teachers of color, obtaining NBC has many benefits, including increased professional development, improved teaching practices, and higher compensation.

Professional Development Opportunities

One significant benefit of NBC for teachers of color is the opportunity for professional development. The certification process requires candidates to reflect on their teaching practices and create a portfolio that demonstrates their knowledge, skills, and accomplishments. Through this process, teachers of color can deepen their understanding of their subject matter and become more effective educators. The NBC process also includes a series of assessments that evaluate a teacher's content knowledge and their ability to apply that knowledge in the classroom. By completing these assessments, teachers of color can gain a deeper understanding of the content they teach and improve their instructional practices.

Improved Teaching Practices

In addition to professional development, NBC can also improve individual and collective teaching practices. The certification process requires candidates to analyze student work and data to inform their teaching strategies. This results in more individualized instruction and increased student engagement and success. Teachers of color who become NBC certified can use these strategies to create a more inclusive and equitable classroom environment. For example, a teacher of color who specializes in English as a Second Language (ESL) can use the NBC process to improve their understanding of the unique needs of English Language Learners (ELLs) and develop specific strategies to support their learning.

Higher Compensation

Finally, NBC can lead to higher compensation for teachers of color. Many districts offer salary increases for teachers who become NBC certified. This not only rewards teachers for their hard work and dedication but also helps to address the wage gap that often exists for teachers of color. A study by the

National Education Association found that NBC teachers earn an average of $10,000 more per year than non-certified teachers. For teachers of color who may face additional financial barriers, such as student loan debt or family responsibilities, this increased compensation can make a significant difference in their lives.

Increased Leadership Opportunities

Another benefit of NBC for teachers of color is the opportunity to take on leadership roles within their schools and districts. NBC teachers are often viewed as experts in their field and are sought out to provide professional development and mentorship to their colleagues. This not only allows teachers of color to make a positive impact on their students but also on their peers and the broader educational community. By becoming NBC certified, teachers of color can take on leadership roles and become advocates for equity and inclusion in education.

BENEFITS TO STUDENTS:
Culturally Responsive Teaching and Increased Student Achievement

The diversity of students in American classrooms has been increasing rapidly in recent years. According to the National Center for Education Statistics, students of color now make up the majority of the public schools' population in the United States. Despite this demographic shift, the teaching workforce has not kept pace. Teachers of color continue to be underrepresented in schools, especially those who have achieved the highest level of certification ---- National Board Certification (NBC).

NBC is a rigorous and highly respected certification process that recognizes accomplished teachers who meet high standards of performance. NBC is an opportunity for teachers to demonstrate their knowledge, skills, and accomplished teaching practices through a series of assessments that include videos of classroom instruction, written reflections, and evidence of student learning. This certification has many benefits for teachers of color, including increased professional development, improved teaching practices, and higher compensation. However, the benefits of NBC extend beyond the teacher themselves, and have a positive impact on the students they teach.

One of the most significant benefits of having teachers of color who are NBC certified is that it provides students of color with more diverse role models. Research has shown that students of color who have teachers of the same race or ethnicity have higher academic achievement, greater motivation, and stronger feelings of self-efficacy. When students of color see teachers who look like them, they are more likely to feel like they belong in school and have a sense of pride in their cultural heritage. This is especially important for students who come from historically marginalized backgrounds, such as African American, Latinx, and native American students.

NBC can also lead to improvements in teaching practices that benefit students of color. The certification process requires teachers to analyze student work and data to inform their teaching strategies. Teachers who are NBC certified are trained to use a data-driven approach to make informed decisions about instruction, which can result in more individualized instruction and increased student engagement and success. Teachers who are NBC certified also have a deeper understanding of their subject matter, which can lead to more effective teaching practices that benefit all students, but especially those who have been historically marginalized in the education system.

Another benefit of having NBC certified teachers of color is that they are more likely to use culturally responsive teaching practices. Culturally responsive teaching is an approach that recognizes and values the cultural backgrounds of students and incorporates those backgrounds into classroom instruction. NBC certified teachers of color are trained to be culturally responsive and are better equipped to create a more inclusive and equitable classroom environment. Culturally responsive teaching practices have been shown to improve student engagement and achievement, especially for students of color.

Finally, having NBC certified teachers of color can lead to higher student achievement. Studies have shown that having a highly effective teacher can have a significant impact on student achievement. Teachers who are NBC certified have demonstrated that they have the knowledge, skills, and abilities to provide high-quality instruction to their students. In addition, they are more likely to stay in the profession and remain in their teaching position, which can lead to greater stability and continuity for students.

BENEFITS TO THE TEACHING PROFESSION:
Addressing the Teacher Diversity Gap and Promoting Equity in Education

Firstly, the presence of NBCTs of color can help to diversify the teaching profession. The profession has long been dominated by White teachers, which can make it difficult for students of color to feel represented and understood. When more teachers of color become NBCTs, it sends a message that teaching is a viable and rewarding career option for people of all races and ethnicities. This can help to attract a more diverse group of aspiring teachers, which can in turn lead to more diverse classrooms and ultimately benefit students.

Secondly, NBCTs of color can serve as role models for students of color. When students see teachers, who look like them achieving the highest level of certification in their profession, it can inspire them to set high goals for themselves and pursue their own dreams. In addition, NBCTs of color can serve as mentors and provide guidance to aspiring teachers of color, which can help to increase the number of teachers of color in the profession.

Thirdly, NBCTs of color can help to increase the cultural competency of the teaching profession. Teachers who become NBCTs are required to reflect on their own teaching practices and identify areas for improvement. This can include developing a better understanding of the cultures and backgrounds of their students. When teachers of color become NBCTs, they bring a unique perspective to the certification process, which can help to broaden the cultural competency of the profession as a whole.

Fourthly, NBCTs of color can contribute to the professional development of their colleagues. Many NBCTs are involved in leadership roles within their schools and districts, and they can use their expertise to mentor and support other teachers. This can include sharing best practices, providing feedback, and helping to identify areas for improvement. When NBCTs of color are involved in professional development, it helps to ensure that the needs of all teachers are being addressed, which can ultimately benefit students.

Finally, the presence of NBCTs of color can help to address the achievement gap. The achievement gap is the disparity in academic performance between students of different races and ethnicities. When teachers of color become NBCTs, they can use their certification to improve their teaching practices, which can lead to increased student achievement. Additionally, when students of color see teachers of color achieving high levels of certification, it can help to increase their confidence and motivation to succeed academically.

In conclusion, becoming National Board Certified offers significant benefits to teachers of color, their students, and the teaching profession as a whole. Through professional development, improved teaching practices, and higher compensation, NBC certification empowers teachers of color to take on leadership roles and make a positive impact on their students and the broader educational community. Additionally, having NBC certified teachers of color in the classroom provides students with diverse role models, promotes culturally responsive teaching, and leads to higher student achievement. As the demographics of American classrooms continue to change, it is imperative that we work towards creating a more diverse teaching profession and providing all students with access to high-quality education. National

Board Certification is one step towards achieving that goal and ensuring success for all teachers and students.

CHAPTER IV

The Journey of Accomplished Teachers of Color:
Challenges and Triumphs

GRAND PACHECO, Ed.D., NBCT

PERSONAL MOTTO:
Loving God, Serving People

HOBBIES:
Reading, Listening to Music

CERTIFICATION AREA:
Exceptional Needs Specialist

What were some of the challenges that you faced in the teaching profession due to your race or ethnicity?

The only challenge that I faced was with making relationships with students because the majority of my students (earlier in my career and in my current position) are different from me. So, sometimes, creating relationships with them was not really a challenge, but one area that I needed to work on. In terms of leadership opportunities, I didn't experience any challenge or difficulty in that area.

Why did you choose to pursue National Board Certification?

To be honest, one reason is the four letters behind your name. I love seeing those letters after my name. I think when you have those letters there, NBCT, you receive more opportunities and privileges. When I became certified, I felt like more blessings came to me professionally. During a recent job application process, I did mention that I am a National Board Certified Teacher and that I have a leadership position in my building or in my district. So, more grants, more scholarships, leadership opportunities, professional development came, and I gained the confidence of my leaders.

When you were completing the NBC process did you face challenges?

Not at all because I had mentors and I had friends who were also pursuing National Board Certification. So, we were in this together. I had support from my peers and also from the district.

What were some techniques or some strategies that helped you to be successful during the NBC process?

Some of the strategies that helped me to be successful were: setting a time to either read, write or research something about my certification area, especially for when I prepared for the testing component. Another one, I had to always be in communication with other candidates, and candidate support providers. When I had questions or concerns, I contacted the school support office, contacted the district providers, and the NBPTS office. Those strategies are very useful.

SHERRY LASSITER, ED.D., NBCT

PERSONAL MOTTO:
Reading Opens Up a World of Infinite Possibilities.

HOBBIES:
Singing, Acting, and Reading

FAVORITE QUOTE:
Education is the most powerful weapon which you can use to change the world. – Nelson Mandela

CERTIFICATION AREA:
Literacy: Reading-Language Arts-Early and Middle Childhood

What were some of the challenges that you faced in the teaching profession due to your race or ethnicity?

One of the things that I recalled was there were some schools that I had interviewed with in the past, and after the interviews, I felt like it went one way, but I didn't get the position or get to be in that school. I have had other teachers of color tell me, Oh, you shouldn't even have bothered to interview with that school, that principal doesn't really hire teachers of color. I found that hard to believe in the beginning because of the demographic that our county has. Then, in this one instance, I went on the school's website and saw their cover picture for the website. Sure enough, there was only like one or two people in the entire picture that were teachers of color. So, I was like, wow! It was eye opening for me. That was very eye opening for me.

Why did you choose to pursue National Board Certification?

Well, for one, I wanted to improve my teaching practice and when I first looked into it, looked at the credentials, what the process brought about and the journey, I knew that I would learn a lot about myself as a professional and a lot about teaching as a profession. Also, it would help me become more of a reflective practitioner, which was something that I was looking for. I was really looking to improve in the profession and I liked the incentive that they were giving. It just seemed to me, like a natural step in my career. The process did make a huge difference in how I think about teaching, how I plan for my classes, and how I taught my classes. When our evaluation process changed to Charlotte Danielson, I felt that I, and other national board teachers who were in the same school building that I was in, we had an easier time adjusting to that process because we were used to having taught that way, the questions that they asked in national board and things that they had you think about and reflect on and do were things that were very closely matched to Charlotte Danielson. The process also helped me as I became a reading leader, as I mentor teachers and help teachers in their profession because I had my experience from national board to draw upon.

When you were completing the NBC process did you face challenges?

It was a challenge in the beginning because it was very different. The way that they have you think about teaching, the questions that they asked. For me, it was very different than how I was trained in school. Even in graduate school, it was very different. It was a very different way of thinking, a very different way of approaching teaching, approaching my teaching practice. So, I had a bit of a challenge just kind of wrapping my head around the process. Also, with the writing part, not necessarily the mechanics and the grammar, but the way of teaching right. I approached it academically, whereas it's very different approach from what I was used to. I sought out support. I went to the support meetings that the NBCT office provided, whether they were in the evening or if they were on Saturdays. I looked at the areas that I was struggling in or where I had a challenge and sought out support in those areas.

What were some techniques or some strategies that helped you to be successful during the NBC process?

Going through the resource guide, the resource materials that they provided, and listening to my mentor was a big, big help. I was consistent with keeping up, not letting the work fall to the wayside, doing my entries consistently. I turned my writing in to my mentor, took my mentor's advice, made adjustments until I felt satisfied and made sure that I had addressed all of the questions. One of the things that I did was to put the questions on the paper as a guide to make sure that I was addressing everything. I did not take those questions out until it was time for me to submit the entries.

SENETRIA BLOCKER, ME.D., NBCT

PERSONAL MOTTO:
Speak, So You Can Speak Again. - Zora Neale Hurston

HOBBIES:
Traveling and Reading

FAVORITE QUOTE:
They Tried to Bury Us; They Did Not Know We Were Seeds. - Mexican proverb

CERTIFICATION AREA:
Literacy: Reading Language Arts

What were some of the challenges that you faced in the teaching profession due to your race or ethnicity?

I became a reading specialist before I was 30. I started teaching when I was 21. I had eight years in a classroom, and then I got a new position. Some of the pushbacks came from my colleagues. The previous reading specialist happened to be white. Our school at the time was literally 50% white, 50% black as far as educators, because there used to be a policy where they were trying to balance out the teaching staff. So, my principal alternated between hiring black and white teachers to keep the staff pretty even. When I was promoted, I think that was a shock to some of my Caucasian colleagues because they saw me in a different role and they saw my growth as a sort of threat to them. This led to some confrontation and some disagreements between myself and other staff members. Another, concern or challenge I had was when I received my second promotion where I was working as a mentor teacher. Some of my new colleagues, who have been there for several years before they hired my cohort, were like "this is how we run things". This is the …, let me tell you…, let me show you. Initially some of the racial pushback I got was "you don't know because you don't know this job because you're new". One incident where I felt like I had a lot of pushback was around the evaluation system. It was a lot of, "well, no you don't know this". In both cases I felt the need to stand up for myself

The National board of certification Journey

and say, "I'm not wanting to, you know, bow down because you're uncomfortable".

Why did you choose to pursue National Board Certification?

Well, initially, my pursuing National Board had to do with an advertisement. I did not know much about National Board. It was not a platform that I was at all familiar with, but when I went to pursue National Board, I had probably been teaching 20 years. My County sends out an advertisement and they said, we're going to pay for you to go through the National Board process. I was like, well, what is National Board? Because, I'm sort of a fad as a teacher. I'm certified as a reading specialist. I'm certified in reading. I've got my admin I, I've got my admin II, but now I'm hearing that there's this national program. I'm like, I've never heard of that, no one has ever talked to me about National Board, so I was like I need to be nationally certified. So, my initial idea to pursue National Board, had to do with the introduction and finding out that there was a national certification. I felt like I should have that.

When you were completing the NBC process did you face challenges?

I faced many challenges during the process. Professionally - my principal. There were three people in my building and my principal literally looked at us at our staff meeting, (three black women, white principal), and said, "You are stupid for doing this. This is much work with national board. Why would you waste your time doing this?" The principal had to sign our letter stating that we could pursue NB, because the county was paying for our national board process. So, she signed a letter to approve us applying, but she was like, "Y'all are stupid. I would never pursue this." So, that was one professional challenge. Just being told that you're stupid for even trying this process. The second challenge was with support. Even though my County offered mentoring support when you go through the process, the lady who was going to be my mentor, who I really thought was excellent, happened to be a black lady. Her mom was diagnosed with cancer and she was an only child. She did work with me at the beginning of my process. We started off in September and around November when her mom was diagnosed with cancer, she couldn't mentor anyone. I didn't have a mentor to take her place. I was still going to social supports that were offered and we still had monthly meetings. So, I continued going to my monthly meetings. I was picking up information and working with my colleagues at my school, but I did not have a person who was guiding me as a mentor. During the February meeting, one of my colleagues and I spoke to a lady who worked for the, district office, and she said, "I'll read your paper for you, once or twice and get you some feedback, but I can't take on the full position." She read our papers one time, gave us really great feedback. She may have looked at our papers twice, but that was all the mentoring I had for the first candidacy. I missed achieving by four points. The second year I went back to finish my process, the County gave me another mentor, even though it was not their policy to give you a mentor as a retake candidate. So, I was able to get a mentor who did work with me the second year. And then a personal challenge was the process. It was extremely daunting. I certified in 2011. So, I started the process in 2009 and I was hoping to certify in 2010. It was just exhausting. Like we did portfolios, our box was due in March, so you're looking at two months less than people have today. I remember from January, until March doing nothing, but just trying to refine type, edit and come up with my entries.

What were some techniques or some strategies that helped you to be successful during the NBC process?

For me, it's just my personality and tenacity in a way. I really, really hate not getting stuff I want. Part of me, was just really like, okay, I've missed by four points, and I'm on a second go round now. I was definitely like; I just have to figure out how to get these four points. Initially I would say other people have done this. I just have to figure out how they did it. What did they do? Who did they know? What did they type? Let me see a lesson, I have to get this, I'm not going to accept that I'm not going to get it. Also, it was the information that I received from going to the meeting. So, one pointer I would give to someone else is: if there are supports offered, like the monthly meetings, you should attend. Talking to colleagues that were going through the process and listening to colleagues who have gone through the process already. You need to talk to somebody, use your resources. Another strategy or technique, you want to have some kind of calendar because you need to keep track of what's due, when it's due and what you're working on. I made myself a chart and I would put down deadlines for videotape, and other checkpoints. If I didn't hit my checkpoints, I knew I had to hurry up or I have to do more with this portfolio and spend more time on that writing. I would also say put in small rewards because it is overwhelming.

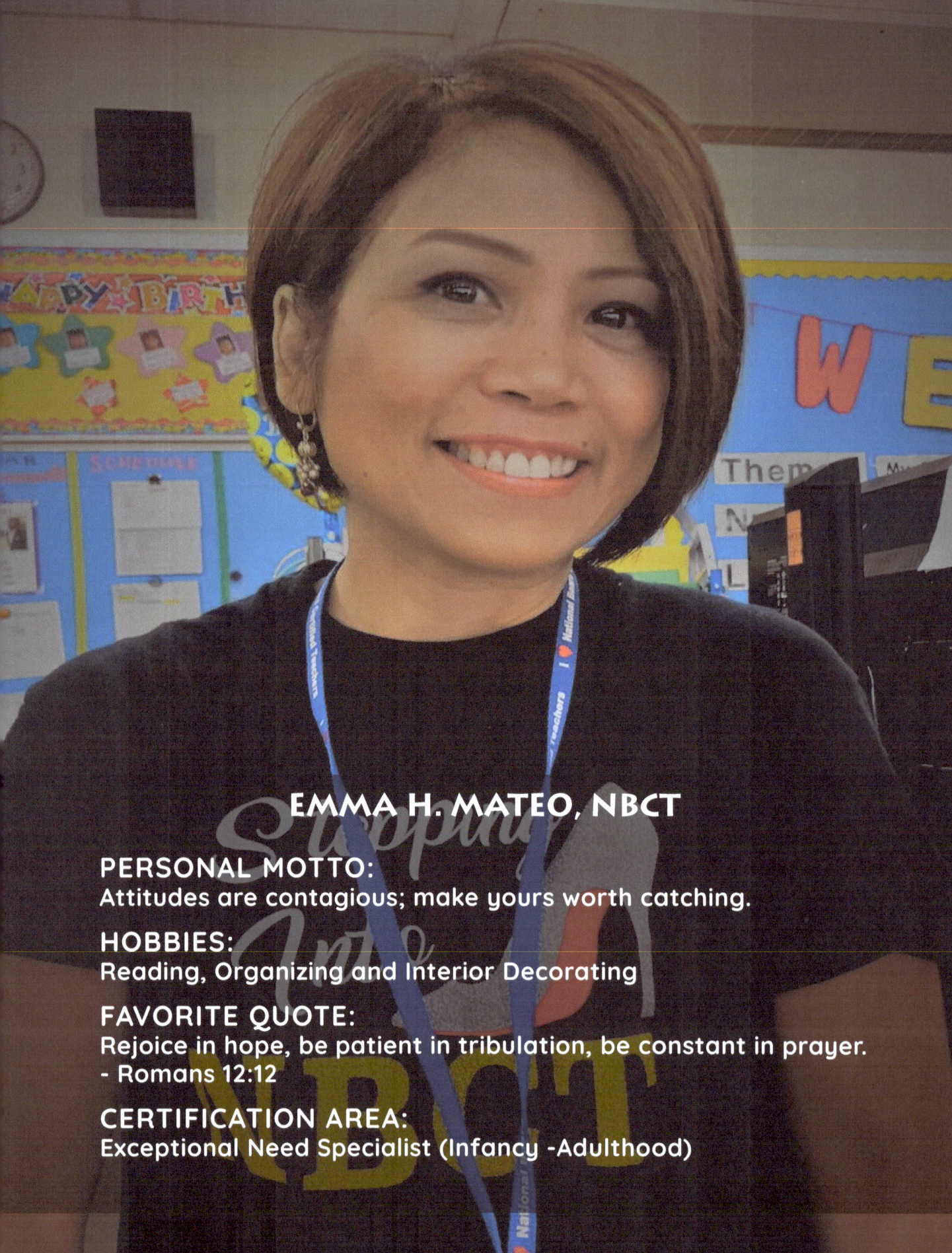

EMMA H. MATEO, NBCT

PERSONAL MOTTO:
Attitudes are contagious; make yours worth catching.

HOBBIES:
Reading, Organizing and Interior Decorating

FAVORITE QUOTE:
Rejoice in hope, be patient in tribulation, be constant in prayer. - Romans 12:12

CERTIFICATION AREA:
Exceptional Need Specialist (Infancy -Adulthood)

What were some of the challenges that you faced in the teaching profession due to your race or ethnicity?

None that were obvious or visible. I would say the challenges came from one's perspective, which varies from one person to another. I came to the United States in 2005. I was naive to invisible discrimination. We don't have much invisible discrimination back in my country, but what is obvious is your economic status. That's where we got discrimination from. Based on that, I anticipated the same when I came to the United States. The discrimination was not obvious and from my perspective, I felt that when I started teaching, I had to learn a lot of things and adjust culturally.

This is my 16th year of teaching in the US, I taught 10 years in the South. There were many cultural differences even amongst States in the US. You see that people have stereotypes. I had stereotypes for Caucasians and African Americans, but I didn't allow them to keep me from developing friends through the years that are in the minority demographics. When I went back to Arkansas to teach it was no longer the way it used to be for me. I developed self-confidence. I already know what I know about teaching, and I know how to ask for help for the things that I don't know. So, when I say discrimination, there is discrimination. Yes. I'm not really the kind of person that gets affected by the stereotypes. Maybe in the beginning years I felt discriminated against for promotion, or leadership capacity. I choose my battles, if it has nothing to do with me being questioned as far as integrity as an educator, I, not going to spend my energy on it.

With all modesty aside, when I've taught in Arkansas, I had been nominated for teacher of the year on several occasions, but they said that what I was doing was not enough. So, after my ninth year, that's when I won the teacher of the year, at the campus and then the district. I was chosen to be a state finalist. There were four of us I was the only minority, the rest were Caucasians. I didn't want to think that it was because I was Asian, but a friend of mine who is Caucasian said they don't really get teachers of the year that are of different color. I did not take it personally, but it was something that was s hared with me.

Why did you choose to pursue National Board Certification?

Whenever I get asked that question, I always try to go back to what were my motivations, my why. I'm that kind of person who always ask why and what. I just ask a lot of questions, but why didn't I know anything about national board. So, when I moved to Arkansas, a close friend of mine invited me. He said there was monetary compensation behind it and coming from a country that is a third world or developing country, that was very essential to me because we send money abroad and other supports. This was my third-year teaching in the school in the United States, so I was really trying to help out financially and to establish my career.

So, that was my primary motivation. I will say that in general, I will speak to the people that came from my country about the monetary compensation. Most of the time I convince them through that, of course I always highlight that's the best professional development you'll ever go through because I've gone through it. After I had my child, I wanted to take some actions on my professional growth. I always want to challenge myself. I asked what else was there in National Board Certification and I was told leadership opportunities if you've gone through the process, and you accomplish. So that was again a motivation for me.

When you were completing the NBC process did you face challenges?

Yes, in all areas personally and professionally. Personally, just because I had just given birth and there were a lot of responsibilities, as the sole bread winner at that time, I had a lot to juggle. In retrospect, being a female, a mother, there's just so much expectations. I woke up

The National Board of Certification Journey

at two o'clock in the morning. That's when I started my day because when I got home from work, I'm also expected to be a mom and a wife. I felt that I was blindsided in a way because I did not know what I was getting into. The friend who invited me backed out and said she couldn't do it. I'm already here so why not? Then I met really good and supportive people in the district and they helped me through the process.

I wasn't able to understand what I was getting into until I was in the process. During that time there were no picking or selecting components. I had to complete them all. In the district where I came from while there is a support group, there's very limited support that they're extending. During my process I was the only one that was going through the same certificate area, so I didn't get the support. I ended up reaching out to platforms like Yahoo groups and Facebook. Most of the people who read for me were from different certificate areas and locations.

What were some techniques or some strategies that helped you to be successful during the NBC process?

This was how I've learned. This is like a mantra to me. The three Rs. You reconstruct, you reform, and you reflect (something that I learned from National Board). Reconstruct is actually challenging. What I believe I already have in my instructional toolkit, the things that I use for collaboration and all. I challenged that and reconstruct. I have listening ears for people who have talked the talk, walked the walk, and who have walked ahead of me. I make sure that I connect with them. That's very essential. After I do some reflection, I ask myself, what do I reconstruct? What do I have to build? What are those concepts that I have to build up and strengthen? And what are those I need to reform. Basically, collaboration and community involvement. My motivation for national board is I know that it will take me to that platform where my words have integrity, where my words can go a long way in terms of advocating for students with special needs or for people with exceptionalities.

VALERIE WHITE JONES, NBCT

PERSONAL MOTTO:
Treat Others the Way You Would Like to be Treated.

HOBBIES:
Crocheting, Singing in Church Choir, Line Dancing, Reading, and Reality Shows

FAVORITE QUOTE:
There is no such thing as failure. Failure is just life trying to move us in another direction. - Oprah Winfrey

CERTIFICATION AREA:
Middle Childhood Generalist

What were some of the challenges that you faced in the teaching profession due to your race or ethnicity?

I would say initially, none. I've been in different schools where the administration was very supportive and the staff was multicultural, so initially did not have experiences of being labeled. Once there was a comment about my Southern accent when I was interviewing for a position. For the most part, I have not run into situations where I was labeled because of my race or ethnicity.

Why did you choose to pursue National Board Certification?

I was excited about the prospect of being a national board certified teacher, because I wanted to move on to another level of teaching. I felt like I was good at what I was doing but I could improve, and if I can improve, I can help my students. So, it was a desire to explore different opportunities and also to improve my craft.

The National Board of Certification Journey

When you were completing the NBC process did you face challenges?

The first thing that challenged me was my fear. I started the certification process during the time when we had to do all of the entries to become certified, not the way it is now when you can choose one or two entries. I was very intimidated by just the enormity of the process. I remember my principal being very supportive and telling me you can do this, you need to get on in here and do this because some of this stuff you're looking for, you're already doing. He really pumped me up. But in terms of the process, it was a lot. Then I found the happy place of incorporating the process into what I was already doing. During the time when I recertified my son was also graduating from college. I was helping him and I was finishing an admin certification program at the same time. I was wearing three hats all at one time trying to certify.

What were some techniques or some strategies that helped you to be successful during the NBC process?

You have to really try to take it in chunks, because if you look at the enormity of everything, it will overwhelm you. I had to make schedules for myself to make sure I did not get overwhelmed. You have to have a schedule. Make sure that you adhere to the deadlines and incorporate those deadlines into your schedule. Make sure you give yourself enough time. Give yourself extra time because you have circumstances that'll pop up. If you have technology, print your work because your computer can crash, you lost the information on your computer and other circumstances. You want to make sure you give yourself enough time in your schedule and through the deadline.

LUCIA CONSTANTINO, NBCT

PERSONAL MOTTO:
Things happen for a reason.

HOBBIES:
Gardening and Cooking

FAVORITE QUOTE:
If you get tired, learn to rest not to quit.

CERTIFICATION AREA:
Exceptional Need Specialist (Infancy -Adulthood)

What were some of the challenges that you faced in the teaching profession due to your race or ethnicity?

There are instances where we were considered ESOL. There's one incident that really stood out when I joined and participated in a countywide curriculum writing for alternate assessment. We were the only teachers of color. The two of us were Asian. It looked like every time we tried to share, we're cut off and were told okay. We were wondering if it was because we were from a certain county or was it because of our color? I just felt that way. I didn't like that experience. They were cutting us off or they weren't really trying to listen to what we had to say.

Why did you choose to pursue National Board Certification?

Actually, it's my principal. Once I started, I wanted to finish it, regardless of how many times I had to retake it. I had to retake it many times. At first, it was just a joke. The principal told me to just join it. A representative visited the school and after the visit, the principal told me to join. I asked why because it looked like it's difficult. My colleague and I said after we finish, we could buy diamond rings. Then we signed up for the process. There were five of us who signed up at our

The National Board of Certification Journey

school, but we ended with two of us completing the process. We had started and we had to finish. We were curious, very curious.

When you were completing the NBC process did you face challenges?

The first challenge was that our principal didn't sign the recommendation form. We couldn't tell anybody. Every time we made a videotape, we had to hide it. We had to do it quickly. Our colleagues were asking what we were doing. It felt like you're Asians and your Filipinos what are you doing this for. We had to show them that though we have different ethnicity we could still do it. Second challenge, I'm not really good at giving details. It also came up in my writing that I always give a general description and it's just not enough. The third challenge was reaching out, collaboration, corroborating with other. I was teaching in a CRI program and it looks like I'm collaborating with my co-teachers and in CRI, and not much with a gen educator. I assumed that they will not understand what I'm doing because they have a different program from CRI. This was not good because I cannot really answer question about collaboration. When I reflected, I didn't really collaborate.

What were some techniques or some strategies that helped you to be successful during the NBC process?

Being open, reaching out to other people and collaboration. I don't ask question unless I exhausted my ways of finding the answer. I rarely asked other people. I think that it's good to collaborate because it's good to be open to other people and to listen to them because when you're open, you're learning more. You can compare what you know, and how you teach and you will realize that there's more to learn about yourself and outside of your classroom.

JULIE HUGHEY, NBCT

PERSONAL MOTTO:

HOBBIES:
Playing Volleyball, Taking Long Walks, Watching Good TV Dramas

FAVORITE QUOTE:
The time is always right to do what is right. - Rev. Dr. Martin Luther King Jr.

CERTIFICATION AREA:
Middle Childhood Generalist

What were some of the challenges that you faced in the teaching profession due to your race or ethnicity?

So, I had to ponder on this one, I haven't really, experienced that much here at what I'll say is prior to coming here. When I was in grad school in Ohio, the population was much different there. I did have some challenges because I had to complete a field experience and I had challenges getting into a school to do that. I can't say for sure if it was my ethnicity, but I just found that people weren't as willing to give me an opportunity to come into their schools. Eventually, I was able to get into one because I had a friend who taught at a particular school and she talked to her principal about allowing me to come and complete my field experience there with him.

Why did you choose to pursue National Board Certification?

At the time that I pursued my original certification in 2008, I was at a school and my team (I had a dynamic team), a dynamic team beyond my grade level, but in my school period. We always were doing a lot of extra things, trying to go to extra PD, trying to learn new information, all those types of things. Around that time, there was a lot of push for people to pursue national board certification. One of my colleagues said we should go to an interest meeting to see what this is about. That's what we did. We went to an interest meeting and once we got there, we were like "yes", this was what we're going to do. It just seemed like this was what all of the best teachers were going to do, and this is what would make us elite teachers. We decided to do it together. There were at least two of us who went through the process together and it was just kind of our team doing professional development together. That's kind of how I got to national board certification. While I was going through the process, there were lots of supports because we had our monthly meetings where we went all the time. Outside of my friend who we were doing this together, there were lots of other people that I ended up meeting and I ended up working with through the process. It was just kind of like a team.

When you were completing the NBC process did you face challenges?

I did have challenges, but I feel like it was time management. Managing my time was a challenge just because there were so many things going on at the same time. Of course, in the school house is always busy and we were always involved in everything. So, if there was an extra event going on, we were helping. It was trying to manage all of that and still go through the process while managing to really put in the time to analyze our work, analyze our practice and do all the things with fidelity. That was probably the biggest challenge, time management.

What were some techniques or some strategies that helped you to be successful during the NBC process?

Eventually I realized that I had to map out a strategy. Once I actually did that, because they were telling us do this, do this, but I was like, okay, I think I got it. I was kind of just going along. Eventually I was like this isn't working. I actually had to sit down and write it all out. Get out the chart paper, plan a calendar, plan a strategy for what I was going to do and when I was going to do it. Once I did that, I found that I was more successful and able to go through the process more fluidly.

ZAHAVA JOHNSON, NBCT

PERSONAL MOTTO:
To whom much is given, much is required.

HOBBIES:
Swimming, Reading, Cruising

FAVORITE QUOTE:
The function of education is to teach one to think intensively and to think critically. Intelligence plus character-that is the goal of true education. -Martin Luther King, Jr.

CERTIFICATION AREA:
Early Childhood Generalist

What were some of the challenges that you faced in the teaching profession due to your race or ethnicity?

As a teacher of color, I feel as though I can connect more with the student population. Only one time did I face challenges when I worked in a school that was predominantly white, and I was the only teacher of color at that school. I feel as though I had to talk a lot about black history month and different people of color that are important. I also feel like a lot was placed on my shoulders to explain about people of color to some of the other teachers. So, that was a difficult situation. I feel as though if you want to do well in your profession, you just have to work hard, study, do the best that you can do, to prove yourself. When you talk to different people who are not of color, I think there's a higher pressure on you to show that you are as educated or as intelligent as they are. I don't think they expect that. So, I would just put that out there.

Why did you choose to pursue National Board Certification?

Well, I always saw those wonderful flyers at my school that were sent out when I was working. The office would send out the flyers about becoming an accomplished teacher, and I really thought about it. I said, you know, that's something that if it could help me become a better teacher, this is something that I would want to work on just to strengthen my practice.

So, it's something that I put in my application for hoping that I would get accepted. Then when I got accepted, one of my friends was like, go ahead, do it, you know, just go for it. I'm like, it's a lot of work, and they were like, no, just go for it. Just try, just try and do it. So, I tried and I put everything into it and it was a really great process.

When you were completing the NBC process did you face challenges?

Well, there was a huge workload. I'm not really that tech savvy. So, at the end, I almost gave up because it was difficult to get my products in, but luckily, my family was very supportive and said no, you came this far, we're gonna help, we're gonna give you the support you need to try to get the work done. So, just getting the work in technologically, was kind of difficult for me. I just tried to stay focused and I tried to get the work in. So that's what I worked on at the time. The second part was a little bit hard. It was about time management. Working through all of the different components was a challenge, but I tried to stick to that.

> **What were some techniques or some strategies that helped you to be successful during the NBC process?**

My mentor always suggested to read up on the process, to stay abreast of what I was to read. So, I tried to study an hour a day or, two hours, every three days. I just tried to keep myself immersed in the process. Then, my mentor would check in with me a lot and see what I had completed or was working on. She had a style that was very direct, and that worked well with me.

MBULWA MUSYOKI, NBCT

PERSONAL MOTTO:
The Sky is the Limit.

HOBBIES:
Traveling to new places, Hiking, DIY, Painting, Cooking, Trying out new things and Reading.

FAVORITE QUOTE:
Education is the most powerful weapon which you can use to change the world. -Nelson Mandela

CERTIFICATION AREA:
Exceptional Needs Specialist

What were some of the challenges that you faced in the teaching profession due to your race or ethnicity?

I would call myself a double minority, dual minority as they say. One being a black woman and then also being from a different culture, that puts me in a different situation. And I always feel that I have to do more to prove myself. When people hear the accent, they may assume that I may not know what I need to know. That has given me the momentum to always check all the boxes, cross all Ts and dot myIs.

Why did you choose to pursue National Board Certification?

I wanted a challenge and I felt that I had always wanted to do national board certification. When I moved from a different state, (I lived in Michigan and I wanted to do it there) I realized that I had to wait until I was tenured at least three years before I could complete the process. I kind of forgot it for a while. Then I realized my teaching was kind of borderline national board. So, I told myself, I might as well just go for the process just to change my practice and make my teaching a little bit more fun. I just wanted something different for myself and for my students.

The National Board of Certification Journey

When you were completing the NBC process did you face challenges?

I did but I had a very supportive mentor. I was a special education teacher and the special education team chair. My administrator at the time was one of those people who did not like conflict. I think that year she decided to start picking on me. I was given more testing loads than everyone else. For example, I had 10 students to test while everybody else had none. She interrupted my class while I was doing the video component and I had to redo it. It was just so many hurdles that I had to jump through. It felt as though that particular year was set up for me to fail, but I pushed through because I could see the end in sight. That particular two-year period was a little bit challenging. I set goals to help make it through. I always used to look at my goals and tell myself you are gold. For gold to be separated from the regular metals it has to go through a very intense heat process. So, at that time, I likened myself to being a gold medalist and I told myself that the things I was going through was part of the process. That helped me hang in there and gave me stamina to overcome situations. Whenever I go through a hard patch, I always reminded myself of that analogy because it helped me overcome that barrier.

What were some techniques or some strategies that helped you to be successful during the NBC process?

I learned how to manage my time. I'm a procrastinator at times, so that helped me stay on board. I'm blessed to have really awesome colleagues who helped me stay on course and, the networking part helped give me different perspectives on things. I also tried to ensure that work and social life were balanced. I was not so much focused on the certification process and the school, but focused on the social aspect of my life. Such balance really helped me a lot.

ELZORA WATKINS, NBCT

PERSONAL MOTTO:
The Solution is in You!

HOBBIES:
Trading, Training, Speaking.

FAVORITE QUOTE:
When you change the way you look at things, the things you look at, will change. - Wayne Dyer

CERTIFICATION AREA:
Mathematics/Adolescence and Young Adulthood

What were some of the challenges that you faced in the teaching profession due to your race or ethnicity?

I didn't experience any challenges with my leaders because the majority of my leaders were black themselves. Whenever I tried to coach, especially in some cases with the Filipino teachers (although they don't say it), because I was black, they didn't trust you. I remember this one teacher she said to me, (I'm not sure if it's because I'm black or because of her positionality as a teacher), but when I first came to support her or to support her school, she said to her peers and to me "why do we need her? I don't see why we would need her." I wondered if I was a white male coming to the school, would I have been able to support more teachers? Because I am a black female, they did not value what I brought to the table, and therefore, they underutilized my talents.

Why did you choose to pursue National Board Certification?

One of the first teachers in our district to become national board certified was always encouraged me. I never knew about national board certification. She was like, "Hey, you could do this.". I was like, "Okay, let me do it." Here I am, national board certified. It wasn't something that was well-known at the time when I certified. My friend suggested it, and I did it.

When you were completing the NBC process did you face challenges?

I had some mental challenges because, national board requires writing, and my content area was mathematics. At the time, I'm thought that math didn't require a lot of writing. That was the scope of math at that particular time. Back when I was in high school, I had taken high level math classes and high level English classes, but when I went to college, I had to take a remedial English class and a remedial math class. When I realized that national board required a lot of writing, I automatically assumed that I was not capable of writing because when I was in college, my writing was lacking, and I had to take remedial classes at that particular time. From the college experience, I had it in my brain that I could not write. I still struggle with that today but I had to develop a growth mindset versus a fixed mindset which helped me work on that. That was a personal challenge that I had. I remember particularly I would go to a local cafe and I would go up there on the weekends and meet with other people who were working on their national board certification. It was so perfect because we would go there in the morning, eat brunch all day, and work on our papers. I remembered looking at this young lady, who was white. She asked if I could look over her paper and I said okay, I can look over your writing. I was thinking that she was white so she can probably write but when I saw what she had written, I realized that I could write as well. Sharing writing gave me the confidence to realize that I could write and I had to overcome the mental block. I told myself over and over that I can write.

What were some techniques or some strategies that helped you to be successful during the NBC process?

One of the things that helped me too was seeing more people like me completing the process. It's like the doctorate concept. When you see people getting their doctorate degree you are like Oh ok, I can do that too. I'm not sure what that's called, but when you see more people doing it, you begin to realize that you can do it too.

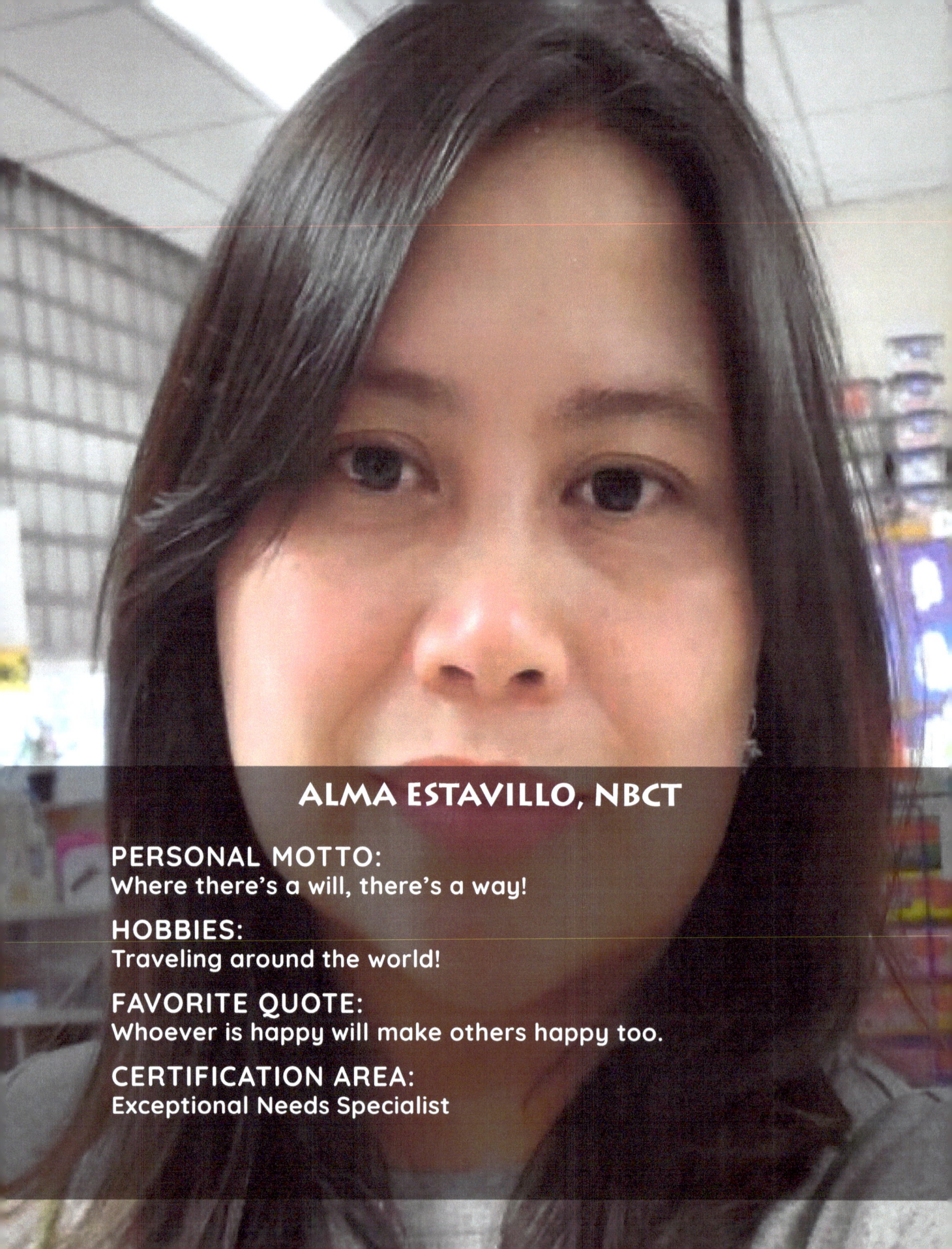

ALMA ESTAVILLO, NBCT

PERSONAL MOTTO:
Where there's a will, there's a way!

HOBBIES:
Traveling around the world!

FAVORITE QUOTE:
Whoever is happy will make others happy too.

CERTIFICATION AREA:
Exceptional Needs Specialist

What were some of the challenges that you faced in the teaching profession due to your race or ethnicity?

When I was new in the country, it was really difficult because of my accent and because of my color. During my three years in Asheville, North Carolina, where all my friends were all white and I was the only one person of color, the principal hired me. But the others treated me like a token. It was really terrible. It was a struggle. My principal and I showed everyone that I had talents and that I had skills. Through my work ethic, I showed everyone that I was a valuable educator.

Why did you choose to pursue National Board Certification?

I chose to pursue National Board Certification because I was just curious. All of my colleagues were like they are giving a stipend plus other benefits for NBC. I began with the Take One and then the coordinator suggested that I complete the four components. So, I decided to complete the four components instead. At that time, I was transferring from North Carolina so I completed the four components and at the end of my journey I felt like I was more like empowered. I tried to reflect during my journey and I made a lot of progress through research and experiments with my students. I felt like I became a better teacher and I felt like it's really a great journey. It helped my teaching skills, strategies, everything.

When I first came to the country, I went from Charlotte Mecklenburg to Asheville. I was different so, my accent and my color made me very shy. I was really scared talking in front of a lot of people. I was so scared. I didn't want to look at everyone to present or share information. When I became a national board certified teacher, it gave me power and confidence. I'm still learning. It's a lifelong learning experience.

When you were completing the NBC process did you face challenges?

The challenges were not professional they were more personal. At that time, we were moving from North Carolina to Maryland, and my principal was very, very supportive. I was going to give up because of the transition, but I received an email that asked when I was going to meet up with a mentor. Then my new principal said, "You have to finish it. You can do it." She kept on pushing and encouraging me. I was exhausted from the move and I got sick moving from one state to another. It was really a terrible journey, but I survived.

What were some techniques or some strategies that helped you to be successful during the NBC process?

Continuous reading. I kept on reading, researching strategies to help my students. Also collaborations with my other colleagues helped me a lot. Also parents support they're very accommodating in terms of the students' needs were and how they could support them. I kept on asking them what strategies helped them the most and what they believe was needed for the child to really succeed. They were very helpful. I had a lot of good parent involvement.

THOMAS PIERRE, NBCT

PERSONAL MOTTO:
I can do all things through Christ

HOBBIES:
Singing, Dancing, and Traveling

CERTIFICATION AREA:
EMC Vocal Music

What were some of the challenges if any that you faced in the teaching profession due to your race or ethnicity?

I think that sometimes not only with white Americans, but with black Americans, they felt that even though I'm a national board certified teacher, that my white counterparts were able to do a more effective job. I've experienced that. I think sometimes in certain situations, I have been given an opportunity because there were so few African-American males in a particular marginalized category that either had no other choice, but had to present or contribute to something.

Why did you choose to pursue National Board Certification?

I wanted to reach the pinnacle of success in teaching. I thought that teaching is an art, a science, and a gift. I love teaching so much and I'm so passionate about teaching that I wanted to reach the highest symbol of excellence in teaching. I heard about national board years before I went through the process because a woman in Washington D.C. was talking about her experience as a national board teacher, how she was able to call the shots.

The National Board of Certification Journey

I just was so intrigued by that, that I called the school board and talked to them about national board, but they didn't really have a national board program. When I heard that my teaching had to be videotaped and it was such a challenging process, it really made me become more interested, more intrigued. Years later, I participated in a program at the Charter School called the "Professors' round table", where I was exposed to national board certification again in Atlanta at a national board for professional teaching standards conference. Ever since that exposure, I was hungry and thirsty to become a national board certified teacher and now I am.

When you were completing the NBC process did you face challenges?

The challenges that I faced were in D.C. I went through the process in D.C. and I achieved my aim after I transferred to Prince George's County. The challenge that I faced in D.C. was there wasn't a candidate support network. So, I had to get help online from people and other candidates or NBCTs who just wanted to help me and support candidates. There are no challenges now in 2022, because you can always find a national board certified teacher in your discipline, and the, the network is so strong. On the other side of the process, the barrier was just the assessment. To me on the examination a lot of questions were ambiguous. I had to take the assessment at least three times. The third time I overcame the barrier by getting recommended books on how to compose music, using Orff. I also needed to see information on music in written form because it's been so long since I graduated from college.

What were some techniques or some strategies that helped you to be successful during the NBC process?

Well, I was fortunate to be able to write well and what I mean by writing well is being a reflective writer. I was glad to find out that transparency was a critical component of the assessment process. Every flexor was a critical part of national board certification. That was able to help me because it was easier for me to talk about where I needed help. The very first thing a person should do is know their standards. Know their standards inside and out. I mean, you may not have to know it verbatim, but just really be familiar with the standards. If you're creating a lesson or writing, you can say this is something that is in the standards of national board. After you become familiar with the standards, then answer the question, don't add anything to it, make it as simple as possible. Once you answer your questions, attach your standards to your why. Once you get a hang of doing that, the journey becomes a little less challenging in your writing.

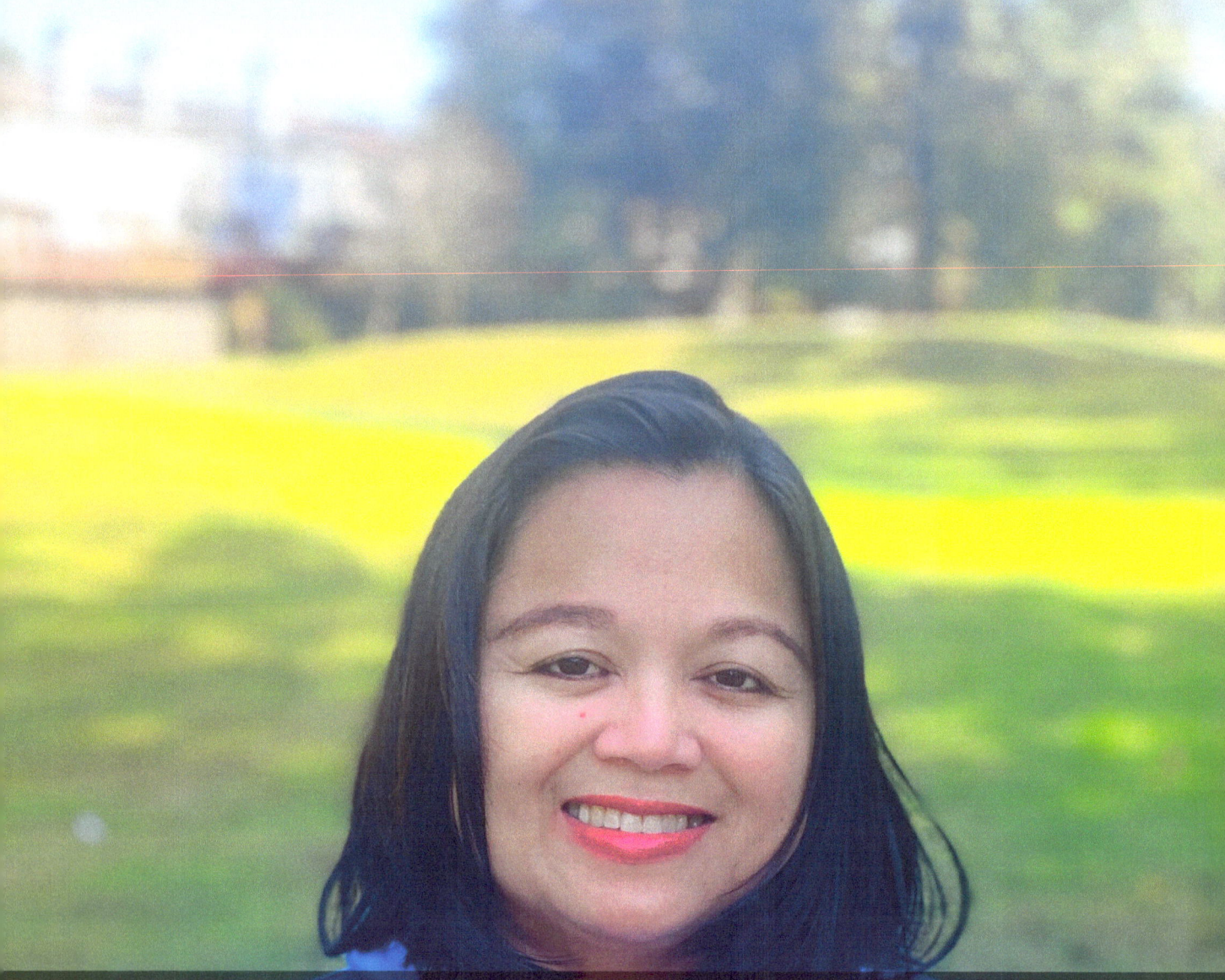

MARICEL BUSTOS, NBCT

PERSONAL MOTTO:
Happiness is a choice. Optimism is a choice. Whatever choice you make makes you. Choose wisely.

HOBBIES:
Kayaking and Arts/Crats

FAVORITE QUOTE:
Every student can learn! Just not on the same day or the same way.

CERTIFICATION AREA:
Exceptional Needs Specialist 2012, maintained 2022

What were some of the challenges that you faced in the teaching profession due to your race or ethnicity?

Yes. You knowing 2006, when I came here to teach in Maryland, I thought I am already like a competent teacher, but there were some parents and even some colleagues who questioned my teaching. They questioned if I am worthy to teach their children and their students. People need to understand. When you are a teacher of color, you have to work twice as hard in order to prove your competency as being a teacher. Eventually, when I realized that there were parents and some of colleagues asking about my competency, I stopped and reflected. Through my reflection I identified a need that needed to address. That need was to validate my teaching profession.

Why did you choose to pursue National Board Certification?

After my reflection, I thought of going through the national board journey in order for my teaching to be validated by peers. I am a teacher of color with a strong accent. I have peers that I wanted to look at my teaching practice and tell me if I'm doing it based on the guidelines set by the National Board for Professional Teaching Standards.

When you were completing the NBC process did you face challenges?

Definitely. The challenge was time management. No one said that it's going to be an easy process. Everyone said it is a process that will change me and my teaching career. Knowing this, I definitely had to work on my time management. I had to ask my husband to do some of the chores or responsibilities of being a mother for me to take the time to write about and go through the certification process in general. Okay. My administrators at the time and my colleagues were very supportive of teachers who were going through national board process.

What were some techniques or some strategies that helped you to be successful during the NBC process?

First, you have to recognize that national board will present the requirements for the different components. Initially, you will think you don't know what to do, but come to realize that they are asking you to specifically apply the NBPTS standards to what you are doing. Once you are in the process, you will have support and you should use the supports that have been provided. For example, mentors are being provided and monthly meetings are being provided, take the opportunity to join them and take the time because that is part of your process. National board is the best professional development that you're going to have, so take those opportunities to grow as an accomplished teacher.

JUSTIN K. ROBINSON, NBCT

PERSONAL MOTTO:
Be Excellent.

HOBBIES:
Home Renovation, and Cooking.

FAVORITE QUOTE:
The function of education is to teach one to think intensively and to think critically. Intelligence plus character - that is the goal of true education. - Rev. Dr. Martin Luther King, Jr.

CERTIFICATION AREA:
Early Adolescence Mathematics (2017)

What were some of the challenges that you faced in the teaching profession due to your race or ethnicity?

Working in the district where I am, there's a lot of minority teachers and diverse students, so racial challenges have not been much of a concern. For the last nine years, I worked in a building where most of the teachers and most of the students and families look like me. I think that kind of gave me a different perspective than a lot of teachers of color might have in the profession. In my new school the teaching staff is way more diverse. Not just black and white but lots of other races. My students were English language learners, not just Hispanic either, but African students who spoke French, Asian students, Indian-Pakistanis, it's a different dynamic. I wonder how that felt when I got back in a school building. Being a minority teacher. I don't think I've ever really felt like a minority teacher in my building.

Why did you choose to pursue National Board Certification?

I'm a nerd at heart and I like being in school. I had finished my master's and I didn't think I was ready to go back for my doctorate degree. I was kind of in a middle ground of enjoying being a student and trying to prove my capacity and my capabilities. I liked that aspect of the process. I was motivated to complete the process because not a lot of people had done it. I think makes it stand out for me. It's not elusive, but it is a distinction. When I see people put NBCT behind their name, I'm just like, that is a thing. If somebody else could do it, I could do it.

When you were completing the NBC process did you face challenges?

The workload was very different. That year was my second year of teaching self-contained. I had all four subjects to teach. Wait, no, that was my second year. Balancing the work, being a teacher of everything was a challenge. Then trying to finish the process. My first year in the process, all of the components weren't ready to be completed. That was a difference, but in general, just starting the program was hard. It was hard wrapping my mind around everything that had to be done. I knew that I wanted to achieve the first time. I didn't want to have to do it again. I'm a procrastinator at heart so it was hard for me to not procrastinate in regards to the deadline. As far as support within my building, it was good. I was single at the time. I didn't have as many responsibilities and the process seemed to fit within my lifestyle at the time.

What were some techniques or some strategies that helped you to be successful during the NBC process?

The candidate support part first. I thought that I would start with supporting myself. It was a mindset kind of thing. I hear a lot of people say I'm not that good of a student and it has been a long time since I've been in school. I heard statements like that. I just thought what was I going to do about it, and I can't worry about the negative parts and the challenges you could have. So that's like a personal motivation thing. I also think people should know themselves and their work style. If you need to work with people then get a cohort. Attend the sessions, meet with others. On the other hand, if you prefer to work alone, just work it out.

In the beginning of my process I tried to force myself to do what everybody was saying to do. I know what I needed so I was just in the quiet room working. That helped me. I needed to learn that was my style. Another strategy that I used was to be realistic about time commitments. Some people have to block things off by time. For example, every Saturday I'm going to work on this or spend time on that. For me I worked on big chunks at a time. I might not work on it every single week, but I might sit down one Saturday and plan to write five pages. It's just like knowing yourself at this point, you should know how you learn and work best, so you block off the time. Finally,

I followed the instructions. The instructions were very dense, there was a lot of information that NBPTS was looking for. So, we should know how to close read and do what we were asked to do. Chunk the work and follow the directions, this will keep you from getting overwhelmed.

JESSICA OLFUS, NBCT

PERSONAL MOTTO:
Be great

HOBBIES:
Crochet and painting

FAVORITE QUOTE:
Live as though life was created for you - Maya Angelou

CERTIFICATION AREA:
English as a New Language

The National Board of Certification Journey

> **What were some of the challenges that you faced in the teaching profession due to your race or ethnicity?**

From my first day as a teaching student, I was the only minority in my teaching program throughout the entire two years. This made it difficult to collaborate and grow because I had to do it alone. Once I graduated and became a teacher, many times general education teachers thought I was an aide or paraprofessional because there aren't many teachers who look like me. They would ask me to do things that they did not ask my colleagues to complete like sit with students that were not on my caseload. As a teacher who speaks Spanish I was also asked to translate frequently although that is not part of my job and was not provided extra compensation. I was asked to translate not just at meetings but also homework, parent notes, assignments, etc. One time I was asked to translate an indigenous language from a country I am not from. and they could not understand why I did not know it and why I could not speak with the new student who was not on my caseload.

Why did you choose to pursue National Board Certification?

I initially chose to pursue National board certification because my mentor was certified and thought I would be a good candidate. Once I began the process, I realized it was a huge undertaking but I wanted to complete it because I wanted to have the confidence that I was accomplished. Many times in my profession I doubted my opinion because it was different than what the other teachers recommended but completing the process made me back up my opinion with research based practices so I knew that what I was saying had merit.

When you were completing the NBC process did you face any challenges?

I faced many challenges but luckily, I found my support team that gave me the confidence to finish the process. I doubted my writing but being able to back it up and have the confidence to know I was doing what research deemed necessary and armed with my knowledge of students, I knew I was doing the right thing. This was backed up with data so it really taught me how to know make sure I am impacting my students and how there are so many little things that make great teaching. Another hurdle was trying to work and earn my Master's degree at the time hindered how much time I could dedicate but I realized that my courses and certification all helped me become more efficient in the long run. I overcame the barriers by having a support group at my school. Some had completed certification, some were going through the process and also had some great teachers who just knew how to teach. Having a great mentor and breaking up components into smaller pieces, so I had time to get a good grasp of the foundation of national boards, also helped immensely. Without knowing what accomplished teaching was, the task was so much more difficult, but being able to study the AAT and standards for months before beginning a component made it that much easier.

What were some techniques or some strategies that helped you to be successful during the NBC process?

A tip that I used to be successful was the way in which I wrote. Many times, when writing, we are not specific, but this forced me to explain my practice in a very direct way. I said exactly what I did and why I did it. Many times, in English, we do not speak or write that way and we don't have to state the reason why we do things. This made me think deeply and critically about if what I was doing was correct. Using the standards and AAT in my writing was also something that helped me be successful.

JOY A. BLACKNELL, NBCT

PERSONAL MOTTO:
Reach for the stars! I guarantee you will reach them!

HOBBIES:
Sightseeing

FAVORITE QUOTE:
Don't stop, get it get it!

CERTIFICATION AREA:
Early Childhood Generalist

What were some of the challenges that you faced in the teaching profession due to your race or ethnicity?

When it is time to get students who are harder to manage, I got all of those students. Whenever there were positions that required a whole lot of work with no compensation, I was asked to do those roles. However, those roles that I was highly qualified for and that provided compensation, I did not get the support. To overcome the challenges, I just created my own lane. When there was something that I wanted to do, I went after it, and I was very protective over it. For example, I am the cheerleader coach. I wanted to do cheer club and so I asked for the position, and if anyone else tried to take over the position, I told them no. It's for our younger students and I was the chair.

Why did you choose to pursue National Board Certification?

Someone recruited me very early in my career. I did not think I was prepared for it. I did not think I had certified, so I was really surprised that I did certify. I noticed that through the process, I grew a lot. I grew into who I am as an educator. Through collaboration and reflection, I grew into that accomplished teacher. Now I do reflect, I do make sure that each and everything that I do for my students, every assignment that I give, I have a particular student in mind. I'm differentiating all the time and I'm also able to make those adjustments on the, on the fly. If I have something planned for one student that I think they may like and they don't like it, then I'm able to make that adjustment quickly and allow them the freedom. They have the choice to say I don't want to do that. I would rather do it this way. The process really allowed me to be flexible.

When you were completing the NBC process did you face challenges?

I didn't have any challenge while going through the process. My mentors were so good. When I had questions about anything, they sent emails with direct feedback to help me improve my practice. I took that feedback and I worked on everything that they told me that I needed to do review or look at differently. I researched content and strategies that would help me adjust my teaching practice. My mentors were very honest with me when they looked at my videos and my writing. They told me to be myself when I was nervous while videotaping and as I watched myself, I was able to adjust, reflect and grow.

What were some techniques or some strategies that helped you to be successful during the NBC process?

I believe that the most important strategies for candidates are: to be teachable, to be coachable, and to read the NBPTS documents.

SHONA SANDLIN, ED.D., NBCT

PERSONAL MOTTO:
Be great

HOBBIES:
Crochet and painting

FAVORITE QUOTE:
Live as though life was created for you - Maya Angelou

CERTIFICATION AREA:
English as a New Language

The National Board of Certification Journey

Have you been faced with differences in the teaching profession due to your ethnicity or race?

Yes. Often times, I have experienced being asked by non-Black teachers, to manage behavior of Black students. In those moments, the teachers assumed that I have a magic wand to manage Black student behavior, and they did not need to invest their energy. I have experienced macro aggressions consistently

at the work place. Often times, there were situations where I was asked to prove my work or experience based on the emotions or feelings of my non-white counterparts. These experiences made the work environment more challenging and unsafe for me. I had to consistently have my guard up.

Why did you choose to pursue national board certification?

I decided to pursue National Board certification with a group of friends that I made while pursuing a master's degree. Once we completed our degree, we saw a flyer that was sent out to schools. We all met together and said let's try it together. Currently we are all NBCTs.

When you were completing the NBC process did you face challenges?

When I started the NBCT process, the district NBCT support office was just established. My friends and I had to figure out how to make sense of the process. We really had to support each other. I had personal challenge during this process as well. My mother was diagnosed with lung cancer. My mom was my biggest cheerleader. She tried to offer words of encouragement to me when I didn't achieve certification on the first try. In 2010, the year I achieved my certification, my mom was so happy for me. She told me it was the best news that she has heard regardless of what she was going through. Sadly, she passed away six weeks later, so I was unable to attend the pinning ceremony. I wear my NBCT status in honor of my mother because she reminded me that if "this is worth it, then it's worth fighting for it!"

What were some techniques or some strategies that helped you to be successful during the NBC process?

I was able to overcome the barriers that I faced during my process with the help of my friends (who were also candidates) and the support from the NBCT candidate support office. We were able to support each other by having work sessions, cry sessions, dance breaks, and motivational check ins when we experienced setbacks.

The strategy that I think would be help others to be successful is to use the 20:10 strategy. You will write or read for 20 minutes at a time, and then break for 10 minutes. I would also use a goal checklist throughout the process to reflect through 30 minutes cycles. Some of my mentees that have used this technique have shared that this helped them to be more productive. I would be an accountability partner for my mentees. I suggest setting weekly goals and having an accountability partner/mentee to monitor your progress in meeting your goals.

Rainya P. Miller

CHAPTER V

Enhancing Diversity in Education: Recruiting, Coaching, and Professional Development for Accomplished Teachers of Color

RECRUITING ACCOMPLISHED TEACHERS OF COLOR: STRATEGIES FOR EQUITY AND INCLUSION

One of the most prominent difficulties in expanding the number of National Board Certified Teachers (NBCTs) of color is attracting a broad pool of educators to pursue certification. The educational system's underrepresentation of teachers of color makes it difficult to locate suitable individuals interested in the National Board Certification procedure.

Recruiting teachers of color necessitates a focused approach that addresses the specific obstacles and constraints that may impede educators from attaining National Board Certification. Systemic factors such as institutional bias, a lack of resources and support, and a lack of understanding of the benefits of certification are among the challenges.

Collaboration with historically black colleges and universities (HBCUs) and minority-serving institutions (MSIs) is one technique for attracting teachers of color. These institutions frequently have a large population of minority teachers, making them ideal for recruiting NBCT candidates. By establishing ties with these schools, the National Board for Professional Teaching Standards (NBPTS) can create a pipeline of teachers of color interested in pursuing certification.

Another method is to prioritize outreach to schools and districts with a high concentration of minority instructors. By offering information and resources on the National Board Certification process, the NBPTS can raise awareness and interest in certification among teachers of color.

Furthermore, it is critical to provide information and assistance to teachers of color who may be unaware of the advantages of National Board Certification. Many teachers may not completely comprehend the significance of certification or be aware of the financial and professional advantages that come with it. Offering focused outreach and support can assist in addressing these difficulties and increasing interest in the certification process.

Mentorship and coaching programs are one approach to provide support and collaboration. These initiatives can assist in connecting teachers of color with experienced NBCTs who can guide and support them during the certification process. Mentorship and coaching programs can also assist in addressing the lack of resources that may discourage teachers of color from attaining certification.

Furthermore, it is critical to address structural concerns such as institutional racism, which may discourage teachers of color from attaining National Board Certification. This necessitates a bigger effort to address equity and access challenges in the educational system. We can encourage and support teachers of color to pursue certification by striving to establish a more equitable and inclusive school system.

In summary, recruiting teachers of color to obtain National Board Certification necessitates a concerted effort that addresses the unique obstacles and constraints that may discourage educators from pursuing certification. We can increase the number of NBCTs of color and establish a more diverse and fair education system by cooperating with HBCUs and MSIs, offering focused outreach and assistance, and tackling structural concerns such as institutional racism.

COACHING ACCOMPLISHED TEACHERS OF COLOR:
Cultivating Leadership and Growth

National Board Certification is a hard and demanding process that requires tremendous dedication from teachers. It entails a thorough assessment of a teacher's knowledge and skills, as well as the display of advanced teaching techniques. Because of structural impediments and a lack of representation, teachers of color confront significant challenges in the NBC process. On the other hand, teachers of color can succeed in the NBC process and reach their professional goals with the correct assistance and coaching.

Coaching is a critical component of assisting teachers of color through the NBC process. Coaches provide individualized support to instructors, assisting them in identifying areas for growth and developing improvement techniques. They provide help and input throughout the certification process, from selecting the proper certificate to final submission.

Effective coaching for teachers of color in the NBC process requires a thorough awareness of their specific experiences and needs. This involves recognizing the influence of systemic racism and biases in the education system, as well as their role in molding the experiences of teachers of color. It also entails acknowledging the cultural and linguistic variety of teachers of color and emphasizing the need of including their viewpoints and experiences in the coaching process.

Using culturally sensitive coaching methods is one effective coaching strategy for teachers of color in the NBC process. This method entails using coaching strategies that are attentive to the teacher's cultural and linguistic origins. This includes respecting the teacher's experiences, understanding their cultural viewpoints, and incorporating culturally relevant examples and instructional tactics into the coaching process.

Another crucial part of effective coaching for teachers of color in the NBC process is the utilization of strength-based coaching. Rather of focusing exclusively on areas for improvement, this approach focuses on discovering and developing the teacher's strengths. It entails using positive feedback to reinforce and support the teacher's strengths while also serving as a basis for future growth and development.

TOC PROFESSIONAL DEVELOPMENT THROUGH COMMUNITIES OF PRACTICE:
Enhancing Teaching and Learning

Communities of practice play a significant role in supporting teachers of color (TOC) pursuing National Board Certification (NBC). These communities provide a space for TOC to connect, collaborate, and learn from one another, fostering professional growth and enhancing their journey towards certification. Let's explore the importance of communities of practice for TOC in the NBC process and how they contribute to their success.

The Significance of Communities of Practice for TOC:

Communities of practice offer TOC pursuing NBC a supportive network of peers who understand their unique experiences, challenges, and aspirations. TOC may face additional barriers and systemic biases that impact their professional lives, making it essential to have a community that provides empathy, validation, and guidance. These communities help TOC overcome isolation, build confidence, and develop a sense of belonging in the certification process.

Collaborative Learning and Knowledge Sharing:

Communities of practice facilitate collaborative learning and knowledge sharing among TOC. By engaging in ongoing dialogue and sharing their experiences, TOC can learn from one another's perspectives, strategies, and successes. This collaborative approach encourages professional growth, stimulates critical thinking, and expands pedagogical knowledge. TOC can gain insights into effective practices, instructional strategies, and resources specific to their unique contexts.

Within these communities, TOC can discuss challenges they face in the NBC process, seek advice, and receive feedback on their practice. By pooling their collective expertise, TOC can leverage the power of shared knowledge to enhance their teaching and strengthen their preparation for the certification process.

Support and Encouragement:

Communities of practice provide a space where TOC receive support and encouragement throughout their journey towards NBC. The process of pursuing certification can be demanding and at times overwhelming, but with a supportive community, TOC can find the motivation to persevere. Members of the community can offer emotional support, celebrate successes, and provide guidance during challenging moments.

Through communities of practice, TOC can also benefit from mentorship and coaching from experienced educators who have successfully navigated the NBC process. Mentors and coaches within the community can share their expertise, offer advice, and provide valuable feedback on TOC's practice. This guidance can be instrumental in helping TOC develop their skills, refine their portfolio, and prepare for the rigorous assessment components of NBC.

Creating a Sense of Belonging and Advocacy:

Communities of practice for TOC pursuing NBC contribute to the creation of a sense of belonging and advocacy. TOC often face systemic inequities and limited representation in educational leadership positions. Communities of practice empower TOC by amplifying their voices, providing a platform for advocacy, and fostering opportunities for leadership development.

Through participation in communities of practice, TOC can become advocates for themselves, their students, and their communities. By collectively addressing the challenges faced by TOC in the NBC process, communities of practice can promote equity, inclusion, and social justice in education.

The "NBCTs of Color Network" in Washington State is a successful example of a CoP for teachers of color pursuing NBC. This network provides a safe and welcoming environment for teachers of color interested in NBC to connect, share resources, and seek advice from experienced NBCTs of color. The network offers professional development opportunities, such as workshops and webinars, and connects members with experienced coaches and mentors.

The Maryland State Department of Education (MSDE) has formed a network of NBCTs to provide ongoing assistance for teachers interested in NBC. The network includes NBCTs from across the state, including a significant number of teachers of color. Regular meetings, professional development opportunities, and access to expert coaches and mentors are all part of the network.

Conclusion

The NBC process is a key phase in teachers' professional development, especially for teachers of color, who have historically been underrepresented in the teaching profession. Coaching and communities of practice are great resources for NBC support for teachers of color. Effective coaching techniques include culturally responsive and strength-based approaches, while CoPs provide a collaborative and supportive learning environment.

By implementing these tactics throughout professional development, we can help to boost teacher representation.

Professional Development for Accomplished Teachers of Color:

Professional development plays a vital role in supporting teachers of color (TOC) in their pursuit of National Board Certification (NBC). While Communities of Practice offer valuable collaborative learning environments, there are several other pertinent methods that can further enhance professional development for TOCs. This chapter explores additional avenues such as mentorship, networking with peers, school-based or certificate area-based cohort meetings, and online coursework, which provide diverse opportunities for growth and support.

Mentorship:

Mentorship is a powerful method of professional development for TOCs pursuing NBC. A mentor can provide individualized guidance, support, and feedback throughout the certification process. They can share their own experiences, insights, and strategies for success, helping TOCs navigate the challenges they may encounter. Mentors can offer a personalized approach tailored to the specific needs of TOCs, fostering growth, and building confidence.

Networking with Peers:

Networking with peers offers a valuable opportunity for TOCs to connect with colleagues who share similar goals and aspirations. This can be done through formal or informal networks, such as professional associations, online forums, or social media groups. Peer networking allows TOCs to share resources, exchange ideas, and learn from one another's experiences. By fostering collaboration and building a sense of community, peer networking provides a supportive environment for TOCs to navigate the NBC process together.

School-Based or Certificate Area-Based Cohort Meetings:

School-based or certificate area-based cohort meetings provide a structured setting for TOCs to collaborate and engage in focused professional development. These meetings can be organized within a school or district, bringing together TOCs pursuing NBC in the same subject area or certification area. Cohort meetings allow for targeted discussions, sharing of best practices, and collaborative problem-solving. They offer a supportive and enriching environment where TOCs can learn from each other's expertise and receive guidance from experienced facilitators.

The National Board of Certification Journey

Online Coursework:

Online coursework provides flexible and accessible professional development options for TOCs pursuing NBC. Various organizations and institutions offer online courses specifically designed to support NBC candidates. These courses cover a range of topics, such as understanding the NBC standards, preparing for portfolio submissions, and developing effective teaching practices. Online coursework allows TOCs to learn at their own pace, access resources and materials conveniently, and engage in interactive discussions with instructors and peers.

Conclusion:

While Communities of Practice are valuable for TOCs pursuing NBC, there are several other methods of professional development that can further enhance their journey. Mentorship offers personalized guidance and support, while networking with peers fosters collaboration and community. School-based or certificate area-based cohort meetings provide targeted discussions and collaborative learning opportunities. Online coursework offers flexibility and convenient access to resources. By leveraging these additional avenues, TOCs can strengthen their teaching practices, build confidence, and successfully navigate the challenges of the NBC process.

Rainya P. Miller

CHAPTER VI

Concluding Thoughts

ENSURING SUCCESS FOR ALL TEACHERS THROUGH TARGETED SUPPORT AND RESOURCES - CONCLUDING THOUGHTS

As we come to the end of this exploration of highly accomplished teachers of color and their efforts to earn National Board Certification, it is abundantly clear that there are significant obstacles to surmount. In spite of these obstacles, there is reason for optimism regarding the future because we are continuing to work toward creating an education system that is more diverse and inclusive.

The importance of providing mentorship and support for educators of color is a key point that can be gleaned from reading this book. In this book, accomplished teachers of color share their stories, which illustrate the significant impact that a mentor or supportive colleague can have on a candidate's journey toward earning National Board Certification. It is essential that we continue to provide these types of support systems for teachers of color in order to ensure their success and to promote an education system that is more inclusive and diverse.

In addition, it is critical to address the structural obstacles that continue to exist in the education system for individuals of color who hold teaching positions. A lack of access to resources and opportunities, as well as biases and discrimination that are embedded in the system, are examples of these impediments. In order to address these issues, we need to maintain an ongoing dialogue and work toward changing the system as a whole in order to make it more equitable and just for all teachers.

One possible approach would be to raise the overall percentage of people of color who hold teaching positions in public schools. This can be accomplished through the use of targeted recruitment efforts, the provision of incentives such as loan forgiveness and opportunities for leadership, and the development of a curriculum that is more inclusive of and representative of a diverse range of perspectives and experiences. We can provide a more culturally responsive and equitable educational system for all students if there are more teachers of color in the classroom. This will increase the representation of teachers of color.

The availability of specific professional development opportunities is an additional crucial component for educators of color who are aspiring to earn their National Board Certification. These opportunities should be tailored to the specific requirements and experiences of teachers of color, with a primary emphasis placed on developing culturally responsive teaching practices, strategies for overcoming structural barriers, and leadership abilities.

When we consider the future, it is absolutely necessary for us to keep working toward the goal of creating an educational system that is more welcoming of people from a wider range of backgrounds. This includes ongoing efforts to address systemic biases and discrimination, increasing the representation of teachers of color in the classroom, and providing targeted support and resources for educators pursuing National Board Certification. As we move forward with this work, it is imperative that we acknowledge the significance of the narratives and experiences of highly accomplished educators of color and the contributions these educators have made to the educational system.

The pursuit of National Board Certification for educators of color is an essential step in the progression toward an educational system that is more diverse and inclusive of a wider range of perspectives and experiences. In spite of the difficulties that are present, there is reason to have hope for the future as long as we keep working toward a change in the system as a whole and continue to offer targeted support and resources for educators of color. We can make the education system fairer and more equitable for all students and teachers if we keep an open dialogue and stay engaged in the process.

ACKNOWLEDGEMENTS

This book, "Amplifying the Voices of Teachers of Color: National Board Certification Journey," has been a labor of love and collaboration. We extend our heartfelt gratitude to all those who have contributed their time, expertise, and unwavering support to make this project a reality.

We want to express our deepest appreciation to the teachers of color who generously shared their personal journeys and experiences in pursuit of National Board Certification. Your stories are the heart and soul of this book, and your resilience and dedication inspire us all.

Our sincere thanks go to our contributing authors, who brought their insights and expertise to enrich the content. Your commitment to educational equity and teacher development shines through your contributions.

We are grateful for the support and guidance provided by the Prince George's County NBCT Network, the National Board for Professional Teaching Standards, and other candidate support programs and providers across the nation, whose contributions were invaluable in shaping this book.

APPRECIATION

To our colleagues, friends, and families who stood by us throughout this endeavor, thank you for your patience, encouragement, and unwavering belief in the importance of this work.

Finally, we extend our deepest appreciation to the readers of this book. It is our hope that the stories, strategies, and perspectives shared within these pages will serve as a source of inspiration and empowerment in your own educational journeys.

Thank you all for being a part of this important endeavor.

With gratitude,

Dr. Rainya

CONTRIBUTORS

Talitha Simeona Stewart, ME.D., NBCT Contributing Author

Grand Pacheco, Ed.D., NBCT.

Sherry Lassiter, Ed.D., NBCT.

Senetria Blocker, ME.D., NBCT.

Emma H. Mateo, NBCT.

Valerie White Jones, NBCT.

Lucia Constantino, NBCT.

Julie Hughey, NBCT.

Zahava Johnson, NBCT.

Mbulwa Musyoki, NBCT.

Elzora Watkins, NBCT.

Alma Estavillo, NBCT.

Thomas Pierre, NBCT.

Maricel Bustos, NBCT.

Justin K. Robinson, NBCT.

Jessica Olfus, NBCT.

Joy A. Blacknell, NBCT.

Shona Sandlin, Ed.D., NBCT.

APPENDIX

Recruiting teachers of color is a critical step towards creating more equitable and inclusive learning environments for all students. To help school districts in this endeavor, here is a checklist that can used to recruit teachers of color:

Nº	ACTIVITIES	✓
1	Set diversity goals: School districts should set goals to increase diversity among their teaching staff and establish a plan to achieve those goals.	
2	Expand recruitment efforts: School districts can expand their recruitment efforts by attending job fairs and conferences targeted towards educators of color, partnering with local universities with diverse student populations, and leveraging social media platforms to reach a broader audience.	
3	Address implicit biases: School districts should acknowledge and address any implicit biases that may be hindering their ability to attract and retain teachers of color. This can include providing implicit bias training for recruiters and hiring teams.	
4	Create a welcoming and supportive environment: School districts should ensure that their work environment is welcoming and supportive for teachers of color. This can include offering professional development opportunities that address issues of diversity and inclusion, and establishing a mentorship program for teachers of color.	
5	Provide competitive compensation and benefits: School districts should offer competitive compensation and benefits packages to attract and retain teachers of color. This can include offering signing bonuses, loan forgiveness, and salary increases based on experience and performance.	

By following this checklist, school districts can take concrete steps towards recruiting and retaining a more diverse teaching staff, which is crucial for creating more inclusive and equitable learning environments for all students.

The checklist for preparing to mentor and coach teachers of color is designed to ensure that mentorship and coaching programs are tailored to the specific needs and experiences of educators of color. The checklist includes the following steps:

Nº	ACTIVITIES	✓
1	Develop a clear understanding of the needs and challenges of teachers of color in your district or program.	
2	Create a mentoring/coaching program that is culturally responsive and tailored to the unique needs of teachers of color.	
3	Recruit mentors/coaches who have experience and expertise in working with teachers of color, and who are committed to equity and inclusion.	
4	Provide training and professional development opportunities for mentors/coaches to ensure they are equipped with the knowledge and skills to effectively support teachers of color.	
5	Establish clear expectations and goals for the mentoring/coaching program, and communicate them clearly to both mentors/coaches and teachers of color.	
6	Foster a supportive and collaborative environment that encourages open communication and feedback between mentors/coaches and teachers of color.	
7	Regularly evaluate the effectiveness of the mentoring/coaching program, and make necessary adjustments to ensure that it continues to meet the needs of teachers of color.	

By following this checklist, school districts and mentoring/coaching programs can ensure that they are adequately prepared to effectively mentor and coach teachers of color. This will not only support the professional growth and development of teachers of color, but also promote diversity, equity, and inclusion within the education system.

The following are reflective questions designed for school districts and educational entities seeking to create a community of practice to support National Board Certification (NBC) candidates of color.

№	REFLECTION QUESTIONS	✓
1	What are the specific needs and challenges faced by NBC candidates of color in our district?	
2	How can we ensure that NBC candidates of color feel valued and supported throughout the NBC process?	
3	What resources and support do NBC candidates of color need to successfully complete the NBC process?	
4	How can we create a sense of community among NBC candidates of color and provide opportunities for them to connect and collaborate?	
5	How can we facilitate cross-cultural understanding and communication within the community of practice to foster inclusivity and empathy?	
6	How can we ensure that the community of practice is sustainable and can continue to provide ongoing support and mentorship to NBC candidates of color?	
7	In what ways can we measure and assess the impact of the community of practice on the experiences and outcomes of NBC candidates of color, and how can we use this information to continually improve and adapt the program?	

This list is intended to encourage self-reflection and evaluation of current practices and attitudes towards diversity and equity within the district or program. By asking these reflective questions, districts and programs can identify areas for improvement and take proactive steps towards creating a more inclusive and supportive environment for teachers of color.

The following are reflective question designed for school districts and educational entities seeking to support professional development for teachers of color.

Nº	REFLECTION QUESTIONS	
1	What are the specific needs and interests of teachers of color in terms of professional development, and how can they be best addressed?	✓
2	What resources and support are currently available for teachers of color in the district, and what gaps need to be filled?	
3	How can professional development opportunities be tailored to the unique experiences and perspectives of teachers of color, and how can their input be incorporated into the planning process?	
4	What strategies can be used to promote and encourage participation in professional development opportunities among teachers of color?	
5	How will the effectiveness of professional development opportunities for teachers of color be measured and evaluated, and what adjustments will be made based on feedback and outcomes?	
6	What partnerships and collaborations can be established with community organizations and other stakeholders to enhance and expand professional development opportunities for teachers of color?	
7	How can the district foster a culture of ongoing learning and growth among all educators, with a particular emphasis on supporting the needs and goals of teachers of color?	

This list is intended to encourage self-reflection and evaluation of current practices and attitudes towards diversity and equity within the district or program. By asking these reflective questions, districts and programs can identify areas for improvement and take proactive steps towards creating a more inclusive and supportive environment for teachers of color.

www.ingramcontent.com/pod-product-compliance
Lightning Source LLC
Chambersburg PA
CBHW041522220426
43669CB00002B/21